That I May Know Him

A Women's Bible Study

JUNE KIMMEL

BJU PRESS

Greenville, South Carolina

The fact that materials produced by other publishers may be referred to in this volume does not constitute an endorsement by BJU Press of the content or theological position of materials produced by such publishers. The position of BJU Press, and of Bob Jones University, is well known. Any references and ancillary materials are listed as an aid to the student or the teacher and in an attempt to maintain the accepted academic standards of the publishing industry.

All Scripture is quoted from the Authorized King James Version.

"Around the Corner, Around the World." Used by permission, Majesty Music, Inc.

That I May Know Him: A Women's Bible Study

June Kimmel

Design by Jamie Miller

Composition by Melissa Matos

Printed in the United States of America

ISBN 1-59166-383-0

15 14 13 12 11 10 9 8 7 6 5 4 3

To my loving husband, David,
for his unwavering confidence,
unending encouragement,
and unreserved support
as I put my teaching into writing

CONTENTS

PREFACE

Jeremiah 9:24

But let him that glorieth glory in this, that he understandeth and knoweth me, that I am the Lord which exercise lovingkindness, judgment, and righteousness, in the earth: for in these things I delight, saith the Lord.

The Word of God, His saving grace, and ministry to people surround my earliest memories of growing up in a pastor's home. I came to know the Lord as my personal Savior as a five-year-old. By His loving grace, I have never doubted that He saved me that day as I knelt by my mother's side in the kitchen of the little parsonage of the Baptist church that my dad pastored.

I grew up with the stories of the Bible. The characters of God's Word were like familiar friends that gave me insight and meaning to the biblical principles I was learning. But through the course of my walk with the Lord, my desire to know God and to study His Word has continually grown. In II Peter 3:18 Paul commands us to "grow in grace, and in the knowledge of our Lord and Saviour Jesus Christ." This verse became the key to my life, to my teaching, and now to my writing.

I've found that the same Bible characters that taught me of God's love as a little girl still have lessons for me to learn. Their lives show me of God's goodness and love, His mercy and grace, His care and provision—all the things I need for this life. But they teach me something more. These dear women of the Bible show me not only how God worked in their lives but also Who God is.

Hebrews 13:8 states, "Jesus Christ the same yesterday, and to day, and for ever." The God of the Bible is the same God we serve today. In this life, we will never be able to fully comprehend the greatness of our God, but one day we will be with Him and see Him as He is. Until that day, let's strive together to know Him better through the study of His Word. Let's look at the truths God has for us from these women's lives in order that we may know Him better and obediently follow His example.

A Heart to Know Him

Jeremiah 24:7

And I will give them an heart to know me, that I am the
Lord: and they shall be my people, and I will be their God:
for they shall return unto me with their whole heart.

Thank you for joining me in this study of God's Word. *That I
May Know Him* is divided into twelve lessons. The three women of
the Bible that we will look at will give us insight into the character
of God. They each had a lowly life touched by a loving God. The
Bible passages that you will study tell about these women and the
events of their life. Read the lesson passages carefully and answer
the questions based on the Bible account. You will learn four
truths about God that each woman's life illustrates. The exercises
will take you to other Bible verses that will help you to further
understand each truth. Answer each question based on the verses
given.

Each lesson, or "Truth," will take about thirty minutes to com-
plete. Within each "Truth" are sections that can be used if shorter
divisions are needed. The key to spiritual growth is to consistently
spend time in the Word. The length of study time will vary with
your other responsibilities. Mothers with little children may be
able to take only a short time with the Lord before the interrup-
tions come; for others the study time may be limitless. The goal is
to be consistent. Be sure God gets a special part of each day!

At the end of each lesson you will be asked in the "That I May
Know Him" section to apply what you've learned to your daily life.

Take time to prayerfully consider how this truth about God should change your day—your attitudes, your responses, your decisions, your words, your thoughts. The challenges you face vary day by day, minute by minute; but God never changes.

I've shared my heart within the context of our study. I've found that God desires to be a part of each moment of my life. He is there to encourage, guide, teach, correct, and love me. These "Truths" are not random doctrines that I've chosen but principles that God has proved in my life, as well as in the lives of these dear Bible women. My desire is for you to grow in your knowledge of your Lord and Savior through our study together.

Join me now as we begin. May the Lord bless our time in His Word!

Philippians 3:10

That I may know Him, and the power of His resurrection, and the fellowship of His sufferings, being made conformable unto His death.

one

MY GOD WHO SEES
Genesis 16 and Genesis 21:1–21

The first eleven chapters of Genesis tell the beginning of mankind. God gives us a glimpse of creation and the early years of the world. But at the end of chapter eleven and throughout the rest of Genesis, we read the history of one family—Abraham's family. Abraham lived in the land of Ur of the Chaldees. The people around him worshiped idols instead of the true, living God. God told him to take his family and leave this land. God did not tell Abraham where to go but simply to go to "a land that I will shew thee" (Genesis 12:1). Leaving required great faith. Sarah, Abraham's wife, faithfully and obediently followed her husband as they embarked for this new land.

God promised Abraham that He would make his name great and his family a great nation. In Genesis 13:16 and Genesis 15:5, God told Abraham that He would give him a family that would number "as the dust of the earth" and the stars of the heavens. Although God had promised that Abraham would be the father of a great nation through a natural-born son, Abraham and Sarah had no children (Genesis 11:30).

After ten years of waiting for the heir to come, Abraham asked God if he should adopt his servant Eliezer to be his successor. This was a common custom of the culture of that day, but it was not the way God wanted to give the heir to Abraham (Genesis 15:1–6). Another custom involved taking a servant to bear the child of the master. Sarah turned to this plan in Genesis 16. She convinced Abraham to allow her Egyptian handmaiden, Hagar, to give him the long-awaited heir.

The simple life of servitude that Hagar had known was overturned as she obeyed her mistress's request. The congenial relationship between Sarah and Hagar would never be the same. But through God's divine plan, Hagar endured to become the mother of a great nation and to meet the God of heaven.

A Servant with a Need

Read the following passages and answer the questions to learn Hagar's story.

Genesis 16:1–4
How did Sarah take matters into her own hands because she was unable to have a child?

_____

_____

_____

Genesis 16:5–6
What did Hagar do for Abram that Sarah could not?

_____

_____

_____

Genesis 16:7–16
Hagar's flight from Sarah had not escaped the eyes of God. How did He make His presence and concern known to her?

_____

_____

_____

Genesis 21:1–14
How did Isaac's birth fourteen years later change Hagar and Ishmael's life?

_____

_____

_____

Genesis 21:14–21
Once again, God met Hagar in the wilderness. How did God give Hagar great grace and hope?

_____

_____

Truth #1
God Gives True Encouragement.

Time in the Word: Read Genesis 16:7–13 and Genesis 21:17–19.

In both Genesis 16 and 21, we see that God Himself is the one who encouraged Hagar. The phrase "the angel of the Lord" is used here and throughout the Old Testament to mean that the Lord Jesus Himself had made a physical, pre-incarnate appearance, called a Christophany. Hagar recognized Him as God and called Him by a name fitting only of God—"angel of the Lord." This is the first account in Scripture of this name being used.

3

Abraham also had an encounter with "the angel of the Lord." Later in Genesis we learn that God asked Abraham to sacrifice his long-awaited son. In obedience, Abraham took Isaac into the land of Moriah to the spot God directed him. Isaac, a teenager, questioned his father when he realized they had the wood and fire but no animal for the sacrifice. Abraham's response showed his confidence in God: "God will provide himself a lamb for a burnt offering" (Genesis 22:8). Abraham bound Isaac and placed him on the altar. Just as he was about to slay his son the angel of the Lord spoke to him. Notice Abraham's response to the angel and the outcome of the incident.

Genesis 22:11–17

And the angel of the Lord called unto him out of heaven, and said, Abraham, Abraham: and he said, Here am I. And he said, Lay not thine hand upon the lad, neither do thou any thing unto him: for now I know that thou fearest God, seeing thou has not withheld thy son, thine only son from me. And Abraham lifted up his eyes, and looked, and behold behind him a ram caught in a thicket by his horns: and Abraham went and took the ram, and offered him up for a burnt offering in the stead of his son. And Abraham called the name of that place Jehovah-jireh: as it is said to this day, In the mount of the Lord it shall be seen. And the angel of the Lord called unto Abraham out of heaven the second time, And said, By myself have I sworn, saith the Lord, for because thou hast done this thing, and hast not withheld thy son, thine only son: that in blessing I will bless thee, and in multiplying I will multiply thy seed as the stars of the heaven, and as the sand which is upon the sea shore; and thy seed shall possess the gate of his enemies.

Abraham quickly responded to the call of the angel of the Lord. His readiness to obey not only spared the life of his son but also brought God's blessing of provision and a great nation through his lineage.

"Angel" of Blessing

Note the circumstances of other appearances of the "angel of the Lord."

Passage	Circumstances	Person's Response	Outcome
Genesis 22:11–17	Abraham instructed by God to kill Isaac About to slay him	v. 11 "Here am I"	God provided a lamb for sacrifice, Jehovah-jireh—God will provide; God's blessings on family
Judges 6:11–16; 22–24; 7:14–15			
Judges 13:3–11; 17:24; 16:30			

Source of Hope

Our world today is full of circumstances that cause fear and uncertainty. It is easy to be discouraged and troubled. We, too, can find our encouragement in God just as Hagar did. Today God uses His written Word, the Bible, to speak to us. As we know Him and His Word, we are then commanded to share His message of hope with those around us. Study these verses to see our source of hope.

I Samuel 30:6—David encouraged himself in _____

Psalm 39:7—The psalmist hoped in God in times of _____

Psalm 42:5, 11—We should hope in God during _____

Psalm 119:81—Our source of hope is _____

Colossians 1:24–27—Our future hope is _____

I Timothy 1:1—Our hope is _____

Promises of God

Too often we become discouraged as a result of our thoughts. According to Matthew 22:37, we are commanded to love our Lord with all our heart, soul, and mind. These passages show a promise that is given to us if we will focus on the Lord. Note what we must do for this promise to be fulfilled in our lives.

Passage	Promise of God	My Part
Isaiah 26:3		
John 14:27		

6

Philippians 4:6–7		
Philippians 4:8–9		

Just a Thought . . .

As a pastor's wife for many years, I attempted at times to carry everyone's burdens. Without realizing it, I would become overwhelmed with all the needs and my inability to meet those needs. It was then that discouragement would set in. On one occasion a dear friend, sensing my despair, slipped me a copy of the words to this beloved, old gospel song. How encouraging to be reminded of God's presence day by day!

Day by Day

Day by day and with each passing moment,
Strength I find to meet my trials here;
Trusting in my Father's wise bestowment,
I've no cause for worry or for fear.
He whose heart is kind beyond all measure
Gives unto each day what He deems best—
Lovingly, its part of pain and pleasure,
Mingling toil with peace and rest.

Every day the Lord Himself is near me
With a special mercy for each hour;
All my cares He fain would bear, and cheer me,
He whose name is Counselor and Power.

7

The protection of His child and treasure
Is a charge that on Himself He laid;
"As thy days, thy strength shall be in measure,"
This the pledge to me He made.

Help me then in ev'ry tribulation
So to trust Thy promises, O Lord,
That I lose not faith's sweet consolation
Offered me within Thy holy Word.
Help me, Lord, when toil and trouble meeting,
E'er to take, as from a father's hand,
One by one, the days, the moments fleeting,
Till I reach the promised land.

Carolina S. Berg

That I May Know Him

1. What in my life causes me to become discouraged?

2. What should I be doing to make my focus stay on God?

3. Memorize one of the passages from the section on God's peace. Determine today to claim God's promise for peace.

Passage to memorize _____

two

MY GOD WHO SEES
Genesis 16 and Genesis 21:1–21

TRUTH #2
God Sees Us.

Time in the Word: Read Genesis 16:13.

Genesis 16:13 says that Hagar "called the name of the Lord that
spake unto her, Thou God seest me." The Hebrew word that Hagar
uses for God is El Roi, or literally, the "God Who Sees." El Roi can be
further defined as "the One who sees our troubles, gives comfort and
direction; who sees our actions and the motives of our heart" and "the
Strong One Who Sees" (Ward).

God had always seen Hagar. He knew her as Sarah's handmaiden
and later as Abraham's wife at Sarah's request. God saw how she
struggled with Sarah and how she suffered at Sarah's hand. God saw
her there in the wilderness alone and afraid. And God saw the future
that Hagar could not.

What three specific promises did God give Hagar if she would return to Abraham and Sarah?

Genesis 16:10

1. _____

_____

2. _____

_____

3. _____

_____

God had given similar promises to Abraham.

Genesis 12:2

And I will make of thee a great nation, and I will bless thee, and make thy name great; and thou shalt be a blessing.

Genesis 13:16

And I will make thy seed as the dust of the earth: so that if a man can number the dust of the earth, then shall thy seed also be numbered.

Genesis 15:4b–5

. . . He that shall come forth out of thine own bowels shall be thine heir. And he brought him forth abroad, and said, Look now toward heaven, and tell the stars, if thou be able to number them: and he said unto him, So shall thy seed be.

How do the promises to Hagar compare with the ones God gave to Abraham?

_____

_____

_____

What a comfort it must have been to Hagar, an Egyptian servant, to realize that the God of heaven saw her need and blessed her future!

God's Watchful Eye

God was not El Roi just for Hagar. What did God do for these Bible characters and how did He minister to them?

Leah

Leah did not escape God's tender gaze even though she felt alone. She found herself in a difficult situation when she was given by deception to marry the man who loved her sister.

1. How were her circumstances complicated (Genesis 29:28–30)?

_____

_____

2. What did God do for Leah as the result of seeing her need (Genesis 29:31–35)?

_____

_____

Jacob

Jacob knew God's watchful eye when he decided to take his family and leave his father-in-law, Laban. Laban angrily pursued Jacob when he learned of the family's departure.

1. How did Jacob describe his years of service for Laban (Genesis 31:36–41)?

_____

_____

2. What did God provide for Jacob as a result of seeing Laban's deceptive ways (Genesis 31:42–43)?

_____

_____

Nathanael

When Nathanael was introduced to Jesus by Philip, he learned of God's ability to see him.

1. What had Jesus already observed about Nathanael (John 1:47–48)?

_____

_____

2. Whom did Nathanael declare Jesus to be (John 1:49–51)?

_____

_____

God's Loving Gaze

What do these passages teach about God's watching over us?

WHO are His eyes over?

*Psalm 34:15*a _____

_____

WHAT does He see?

Proverbs 15:3 _____

_____

WHEN does He watch us?

Psalm 121:3–4 _____

_____

WHERE does God see us?

Proverbs 15:3 _____

_____

WHY does He watch over us?

II Chronicles 16:9 _____

_____

HOW closely does God Watch us?

Job 31:4 _____

_____

Just a Thought . . .

What a precious comfort to know our God is a God who sees! No matter our circumstances, no matter our burdens, He sees and cares.

We must, however, also be challenged to consider what we see. Do we see God as He would have us to? Are our lives full of facts about God? We've perhaps grown up hearing about Him, but do we know Him personally? Have we allowed the truths and promises of His Word to become reality in our lives? Often it's times of trial and suffering that force us to see who God truly is.

Few have experienced suffering as Job did. Yet at the end of his trials Job said that he saw God. Job admitted to having heard about God, but now He saw God. "I have heard of thee by the hearing of the ear: but now mine eye seeth thee" (Job 42:5).

It was then that God began to bless Job and restore all that had been taken from him. Job's trials had made him see God. How do you see God?

That I May Know Him

1. Do I desire to see God or am I satisfied to only hear about Him?

   _____

2. How will I view the events of my day if I remember that God sees me?

   _____

   _____

   _____

   _____

3. Read Job 42:5 and ask God to help you truly see Him today. Make note of what He does for you throughout your day that lets you see Him more clearly.

   _____

   _____

   _____

three

MY GOD WHO SEES

Genesis 16 and Genesis 21:1–21

TRUTH #3
God Hears Our Prayers.

Time in the Word: Read Genesis 21:9–21.

Hagar obeyed the angel of the Lord and returned to Abraham and Sarah. Soon her son Ishmael was born. Fourteen long years passed before God miraculously fulfilled His promise to Abraham and Sarah and gave them a son.

How did Isaac, the promised heir, change Hagar and Ishmael's place in Abraham's home (Genesis 21:9–14)?

_____

_____

_____

_____

15

Once again, Hagar was in the wilderness of Beersheba, but this time Ishmael was with her. Their getting to Egypt seemed hopeless because their water supply was gone (v. 15). Hagar knew nothing else to do for her son but to walk away and leave him to die. The cries that came from this mother's heart were not unheard by her God. As He had seen her in this same wilderness years before, He heard her this day. God directed Hagar to hold her son and to be reminded of His promises to her.

God had heard both Hagar's cries and Ishmael's voice. Her son's name means literally "God hears." Psalm 34:15 states, "The eyes of the Lord are upon the righteous, and his ears are open unto their cry." As we go to God in prayer, we can be assured that He hears!

Promises of God

What do these passages teach of God's promise to hear our prayers?

1. *Psalm 4:3*—But know that the Lord hath set apart him that is godly for himself: the Lord will hear when I call unto Him.

The Lord will hear when _____

_____

2. *Psalm 10:17*—Lord, thou hast heard the desire of the humble: thou wilt prepare their heart, thou wilt cause thine ear to hear.

The Lord will hear the prayers of the _____

_____

3. *Psalm 66:18*—If I regard iniquity in my heart, the Lord will not hear me.

The Lord will not hear my prayer if I _____

_____

4. *Matthew 6:6*—But thou, when thou prayest, enter into thy closet, and when thou hast shut thy door, pray to thy Father which is in secret; and thy Father which seeth in secret shall reward thee openly.

When I pray in _____, God will reward me _____

5. *I John 5:14*—And this is the confidence that we have in him, that, if we ask any thing according to his will, he heareth us.

If I ask _____, He will hear.

In Psalm 17:6, David declares, "I have called upon thee, for thou wilt hear me, O God: incline thine ear unto me, and hear my speech." David knew God heard his prayers. Why do we at times doubt that God hears our prayers? I'm afraid that too often we question God because He doesn't give us immediately what we believe to be the right answer. He may answer in a different way from what we had imagined. He may respond with a definite "no." Or, He may ask us to wait on Him—the most difficult response of all. The problem is not that God doesn't hear, but that we don't like His answer.

Three Kinds of Prayers

There are different kinds of prayers that we can pray. Some prayers are directly asking God for specific needs or situations. Other prayers come from hearts that are unable to express the needs and go to God in the form of tears or even silent requests that the Holy Spirit must articulate for us. Study these verses to understand better the kinds of prayer.

Direct Prayer

Passage	Person/Group	Specific Need/Request
Judges 6:36–40		
Jonah 2:1–10		
Acts 9:40		
Acts 12:5–12		
James 5:17–18		

Silent Prayer

Passage	God's Help in Prayer
Psalm 139:1, 23	
Romans 8:26	
Hebrews 4:12–13	

Prayer of Tears

Where does God put the tears you shed when you pray with a broken heart?

Psalm 56:8 _____

_____

_____

_____

How does God depict His remembering our prayer of tears?

Psalm 56:8; Malachi 3:16 _____

_____

_____

_____

Just a Thought . . .

When I taught elementary school, I would often give my students sheets of math problems to test their knowledge of math facts. The page would be full of problems—addition, subtraction, and multiplication. But I never gave them the answers—only the problems. The students had to supply the correct answers within the time limits I set for them. This should be our approach to prayer. We need to give our problems to God and let Him within the time frame of His love and wisdom supply the correct answers.

That I May Know Him

1. According to Psalm 116:1–2, how long can we be confident that God will listen to our prayers?

_____

_____

2. What prayers have I seen God answer directly for me in the past week? Month? Year?

_____

_____

_____

_____

3. How much time do I spend in prayer each day? Do I rush through my prayer time or do I concentrate as I should?

_____

_____

4. What steps do I daily take to be sure I come to God in prayer with a pure heart?

_____

_____

_____

_____

5. Spend time right now in prayer. Thank God for His promise to hear and answer your prayers.

four
MY GOD WHO SEES
Genesis 16 and Genesis 21:1–21

TRUTH #4
God, in His Grace, Provides for Every Need.

Time in the Word: Read Genesis 16:8–9 and Genesis 21:17–21.

In chapter 16 we see that God told Hagar to return to Sarah and to submit herself again to Sarah's authority. He did not deny the validity of her suffering and pain, nor did He promise that everything would be fine when she returned. He simply and directly told her to go back to submit to Sarah. God then gave Hagar the incredible promise of future prosperity for her son. God's grace allowed her to go back with the hope of deliverance and great blessing.

How many times do we go to God in prayer asking Him to take our burdens yet He seems to ignore our requests and ask us to continue carrying them? He often asks us to trust Him and continue in our uncertainties as He did Hagar. He does not promise to eliminate our burdens, but He does promise that His grace will always match our needs.

In chapter 21, God did not ask Hagar and Ishmael to return to Abraham's house. Instead He provided for their needs. First, God opened Hagar's eyes to see the well, providing their immediate need of water. Then God again promised great blessings for Ishmael's lineage.

Promises of God

Just as God provided for Hagar and Ishmael's needs, He has promised to meet our needs as well. His grace is sufficient for every need. Sufficient means that God gives us exactly what we need, nothing more and nothing less.

How do these passages apply to Hagar's needs? How do they apply to your needs?

Passage	Hagar's Need	My Need
Psalm 23:1		
Psalm 23:2–3		
Psalm 27:1–3		
Psalm 32:8		
Matthew 6:33		

II Corinthians 1:3–4		
Ephesians 6:5–8		
Philippians 4:19		
II Peter 1:3–4		

Our Daily Needs

In Matthew 6, Jesus spent part of the Sermon on the Mount teaching His disciples to trust Him for their simplest needs. Many times the basic cares of this world can cause the greatest worry because we believe we can supply them ourselves. Our loving heavenly Father desires that we trust Him for all things! To walk in the spiritual blessings He provides for us, we must put our trust completely in Him for all things. Many have placed their faith in Christ to save them from their sins, but they doubt His ability to meet their daily needs.

Read Matthew 6:24–34 and answer the following questions.

1. What two masters do we try to serve?

2. What are we not to worry about ("take no thought for")?

3. If our life is more than these things, of what does it truly consist?

4. What are we to learn from God's care of the following:
    Birds— _____

    _____

    Lilies/Grass— _____

    _____

5. Who knows we need all these things?

    _____

6. What must I do for the cares of this world to be provided?

    _____

Just a Thought . . .

"Your heavenly Father knoweth that ye have need of all these things" (Matthew 6:32). What comfort that verse has been to my heart! When both our girls were in college and our son was in a Christian school, the tuition payments alone could seem overwhelming at times. Whenever I would start to panic at the beginning of a new month, I would be encouraged by this verse. My heavenly Father already knew! Oh, I would still take the totals to Him in prayer and obediently lay them at His feet. But He already knew. There would be times that worry overcame me, and He would gently remind me again—He already knew. He never failed to provide.

That I May Know Him

"Faith is the total confidence in the provision of God" (King James Study Bible, p. 1424).

1. What needs am I currently facing that I need to trust God for?

_____

_____

_____

2. How does my worry contradict the faith that I say I have in God?

_____

_____

_____

3. What should I do when I am tempted to worry about the things of this life?

_____

_____

_____

4. Spend time in prayer right now. Thank God for His promises to meet your every need.

From My Heart to Yours

I have fond memories of going to my grandpa and grandma's farm as a little girl. It had been in my family for several generations and proudly displayed the "Centennial Farm" sign in the front yard. One of the highlights of playing in the yard was getting a drink from the well to quench my thirst. Oh, there was running water in the house, but somehow it didn't taste as cold and delicious as the water we pumped from the well. My sisters and I would race to the pump to see who would get the first drink. I can still see the tin cup hanging on a nail near the pump. It didn't matter to us who had used the cup last or what little creature may have just passed through the cup. It was just part of the pleasure of drinking from Grandpa's well. When I think of the life of Hagar, I remember that well and tin cup. God could have easily provided just a cup of water for Hagar to give her thirsty son, but instead, God gave Hagar a whole well to meet Ishmael's need. Hagar's God is our God. He desires to meet our needs "exceeding abundantly above all that we ask or think" (Ephesians 3:20).

five

MY GOD WHO CARES
John 4:1 42

Not many weeks into His ministry as He and His disciples were traveling from Judea to Galilee, Jesus set an example that startled many of the Jews. He displayed a burden and love for a people that the Jews considered outcasts. Most Jews would have traveled around Samaria to reach this destination, but Jesus chose to go through Samaria. He sat by a well and rested while His disciples went to get food. He knew a woman from Sychar would be making her daily visit to this well. The other women from the area had already been to the well for the day's water supply. Because these women did not welcome her, the woman from Sychar chose to battle the heat of the day rather than face their contempt. Having been shunned and ignored, she chose to come alone. Jesus did not care about her reputation. He waited for her, ready to meet her greatest need.

A Woman by a Well

Read the following verses and then answer the questions. We will learn some precious truths about the Lord Jesus as we look at Him spending an afternoon near Samaria.

John 4:1–9

When Jesus came to the city of Sychar in Samaria, why did He sit down by the well?

_____

_____

_____

Jesus knew this woman would be coming to the well even though it was not the normal time for women to get water. What did Jesus ask of her?

_____

_____

Why was the woman surprised that Jesus asked her this?

_____

_____

John 4:10–15

What kind of water did Jesus offer her? How did Jesus describe this water?

_____

_____

What did Jesus ask the woman to do to help her see her sin?

_____

_____

John 4:19–26

Because Jesus told the woman about herself, who did she think Jesus was (v. 19, 25)?

_____

_____

Who did Jesus tell her He was? _____

John 4:27–30

What message did the woman have for the people of her city?

_____

_____

What did her message cause others to do?

_____

_____

John 4:31–38

What did Jesus want the disciples to see?

_____

_____

John 4:39–42

What two reasons are given for why the people believed Jesus?

_____

_____

TRUTH #1
Jesus Cares for Individuals.

Time in the Word: Read John 4:6–28.

As Jesus was on His way to Galilee, He chose to go through Samaria. Most Jews traveling through this area would have gone many miles out of their way to avoid passing through this region. "The Samaritan people had been despised by the Jews since Old Testament times due to their intermarriage with the Gentile peoples among whom they lived . . . and due to their belief that Mount Gerizim, not Jerusalem, was the place appointed by God for sacrifice" (King James Study Bible, p. 1613). Yet Jesus chose this spot to sit and rest while the disciples went to get food. Jesus knew that in just a short time a woman who needed Him would come to this well. He purposely chose to minister to this woman instead of joining the disciples, where there would be many people. In spite of His weariness, He knew this woman needed His love. Jesus cares for individuals.

Jesus asked this woman for a drink from the well and began a conversation that would change her life. She came to the well at a time when the other ladies of Sychar would not be there. Her reputation and lifestyle had ostracized her from them. But today she would have individual attention from the Lord Jesus Himself. Jesus offered her the knowledge and acceptance not only of the Living Water, the Holy Spirit, but also of the Messiah. While He told her all that she had done, she realized to whom she was talking. Jesus admitted to her what He did not always share with others: He was the Messiah.

In the following passages you will see other times that people asked Jesus who He was. Notice the answers Jesus gave to these people and see how special it was for Him to openly admit His identity to a Samaritan woman.

Passage	Jesus' Answer
Matthew 27:11–14	
Luke 9:18–21	
John 19:7–9	

One by One

Throughout His earthly ministry, Jesus cared for individuals. Even when surrounded by crowds, He never lost sight of the individual lives He was touching. It was one by one that He healed people, even if they were part of the multitude. Read the following passages and note the individuals that Jesus ministered to. Were they by themselves or in a large group?

1. *Luke 8:40–48* _____

_____

_____

2. *Luke 14:1–6* _____

_____

_____

3. *John 3:1–16* _____

_____

4. *John 9:1–7* _____

_____

_____

One Sent to One

After the Lord Jesus was crucified, resurrected, and ascended back to heaven, He still was concerned for individuals who were seeking Him. In the book of Acts, Philip was used by God to preach the truth to many people. Philip was one of the first deacons chosen by the early church (Acts 6:1–7). In Acts 8, Philip was preaching in the city of Samaria. Many people there were listening and accepting Philip's message of Christ. In verse 26, God called Philip to leave the city to go to the desert of Gaza to minister to one man from Ethiopia. The Word of God was spread into North Africa through this individual that Philip spent time with.

What took place in the life of this one man that Philip ministered to?

1. Describe Philip's ministry in Samaria (Acts 8:5–8).

_____

_____

2. What did the Ethiopian man ask Philip to do (8:26–31)?

_____

_____

3. What did Philip preach to this man (8:32–35; Isaiah 53:7–8)?

_____

_____

_____

4. How did the Ethiopian man respond to Philip's message (8:36–40)?

_____

_____

_____

Just a Thought . . .

Can God depend on you, as He did Philip, to share His message of salvation with those around you? In our busy lives, it is easy to lose sight of the individuals that need Christ as Savior. We need to walk closely with our Lord. Then when He asks us to stop our routine to minister to one nearby, we will hear Him and should obey.

Lord, Speak to Me

Lord, speak to me, that I may speak
In living echoes of Thy tone;
As Thou hast sought, so let me seek
Thy erring children lost and lone.

O teach me, Lord, that I may teach
The precious things Thou dost impart;
And wing my words, that they may reach
The hidden depths of many a heart.

O fill me with Thy fullness, Lord,
Until my very heart o'erflow
In kindling thought and glowing word
Thy love to tell, Thy praise to show.

O use me, Lord, use even me,
Just as Thou wilt and when and where;
Until Thy blessed face I see,
Thy rest, Thy joy, Thy glory share.

Frances R. Havergal

That I May Know Him

1. Whom do you know that needs to meet the Lord Jesus? List neighbors, friends, and relatives that you need to reach out to as Jesus did to this Samaritan woman and Philip did to the Ethiopian man.

_____

_____

_____

_____

_____

2. Pray for each person you listed. Ask the Lord to help you make opportunities to witness to these people.

six

MY GOD WHO CARES
John 4:1–42

TRUTH #2
Jesus Cares for the Multitudes.

Time in the Word: Read John 4:31–42.

When the disciples returned with the food, Jesus had just told the woman that He was the Messiah of whom the prophets had spoken. The disciples marveled that Jesus was talking to this woman. The woman then returned to her city to tell her people about Jesus. While she was gone, Jesus refused to eat. He used this opportunity to challenge His disciples to "lift up . . . [their] eyes, and look on the fields; for they are white already to harvest." As they looked up, they no doubt saw all the people from Sychar that the woman was bringing to the well to hear Jesus.

Jesus often used the events of harvest to illustrate the winning of souls. The Greek word used in verse 35 figuratively refers to "the act of harvesting," "the time of harvest," and "the crop" (*New Strong's*

Expanded Dictionary, p. 115). Jesus wanted His disciples to see this multitude with the same compassion that He did. He wanted them to realize these people needed to be gathered as a crop at harvest.

Jesus' Burden for the Multitude

Matthew 9:35–38

And Jesus went about all the cities and villages, teaching in their synagogues, and preaching the gospel of the kingdom, and healing every sickness and every disease among the people. But when he saw the multitudes, he was moved with compassion on them, because they fainted, and were scattered abroad, as sheep having no shepherd.

Matthew 14:14

And Jesus went forth, and saw a great multitude, and was moved with compassion toward them, and he healed their sick.

How would you describe Jesus' burden for the multitude?

_____

_____

_____

_____

Jesus' Care of the Multitude

Wherever Jesus went, the multitudes followed Him. His compassion for them was demonstrated in many ways. As you study these passages, note the ways Jesus reached out to the multitudes. What did He do for them?

Matthew 13:1–2

Jesus _____ the multitude.

Matthew 14:15–21

Jesus _____ the multitude.

Luke 6:17–19

Jesus _____ the multitude.

The Multitude's Response to Jesus

Read the following passages and answer the questions to see the multitudes' response to Jesus.

Matthew 9:8, 33

How did the multitudes respond to Jesus? _____

_____

Did they realize who Jesus was? _____

_____

Matthew 21:1–11, 45–46

How did the multitude honor Jesus? _____

_____

_____

Who did the multitude think Jesus was? _____

Matthew 27:20–25

In just a few days, the multitudes' opinion of Jesus changed. What did the multitude tell Pilate to do to Jesus? _____

_____

What caused this change? _____

_____

Did Jesus' compassion change for the multitude (Luke 23:33–34)?

_____

Just a Thought . . .

How often I become so intent in my own little world that I don't even notice the people around me! I sat in my car at a stoplight recently and tried to see the faces of the drivers as they turned the corner in front of me. Faces came car by car and each face represented a soul that either knew my Lord as Savior or did not. I was overwhelmed. How long has it been since you stopped to look into the faces of the multitudes around you? Do you have compassion for them? May Jesus' words to His disciples challenge our hearts as well: "Lift up your eyes, and look on the fields; for they are white already to harvest" (John 4:35).

That I May Know Him

1. Where do I go that I am near large groups of people?

_____

_____

_____

_____

2. How do I respond to these multitudes? Do I become impatient or do I see them as Jesus would?

_____

_____

_____

_____

3. If I understand Christ's love for the lost (Matthew 9:35–38), what should my attitude be toward the unsaved multitudes around me?

_____

_____

_____

_____

seven

MY GOD WHO CARES
John 4:1–42

TRUTH #3
Jesus Uses Individuals to Reach the Multitudes.

Time in the Word: Read John 4:28–30, 39–42.

The woman left her water pot by the well and quickly returned to her city. When she realized who Jesus was, she immediately wanted to share the news with everyone she knew. She wanted the men of the city to come to see the one who had told her everything she had done. Who else could it be but the Christ that they had heard would one day come? One by one the men of the city heard her report, and soon a multitude began the walk to the well to see Jesus.

The woman did not know everything about Jesus, but she knew enough to tell others what He had done for her. Through her efforts, many from her city believed on Jesus. Some quickly believed Him when they heard the woman's words (v. 39). Others believed when they heard Jesus for themselves. None of this multitude would have come to Jesus that day were it not for the concern of one woman.

One Sent to Many

God often uses one individual to get His message to many. Throughout the book of Acts as the church was being established, God used one or two men at times to proclaim the truth; many came to know Jesus Christ.

In these passages, whom did God use to reach many people for Him? How many people turned to God?

Passage	Person(s) God Used	Number Who Believed
Acts 2:14–42		
Acts 4:1–4	Peter and John	
Acts 5:12–16	Peter	
Acts 9:36–42		
Acts 11:22–25		
Acts 17:1–4		

Acts 17:10–12		
Acts 21:18–20		

Just a Thought . . .

You and I may never influence a multitude at one time as this Samaritan woman did, but our lives do touch more people than we may realize. God asks us to faithfully proclaim and live His gospel to all we meet.

My Influence

My Life shall touch a dozen lives
Before this day is done.
Leave countless marks of good or ill,
E'er sets the evening sun.
This, the wish I always wish,
The prayer I always pray,
Lord, may my life help other lives
It touches by the way.

Author Unknown

That I May Know Him

1. I may not have opportunity to speak to thousands at one time about the Lord, but how would I describe my burden for large groups or regions of people?

_____

_____

_____

_____

2. What mission projects or missionaries do I support that work with multitudes (i.e., inner-city ministries, college campus, camps)?

_____

_____

_____

_____

3. Take a few minutes to pray for these mission works. What part would God have for me in reaching the multitudes?

eight

MY GOD WHO CARES
John:1–42

TRUTH #4
Jesus Wants You to Tell Others About Him.

Time in the Word: Read John 17:18 and Matthew 28:19–20.

Jesus desires that all of us, as His children, tell others about His saving grace. In John 17, the Lord Jesus declares that He is sending believers into the world as God the Father had sent Him. Once a person is saved, she has a responsibility to share the gospel with others.

1. **Be Burdened**—Our sharing salvation with others begins with a love and burden for the lost. We must "lift up our eyes" as Jesus commanded His disciples to do. We must see the needs of those around us. We must share Jesus' concern and compassion for the souls of others.

According to Matthew 9:36 what was Jesus' reaction when He saw the multitude?

_____

_____

What should be our response according to II Corinthians 5:14?

_____

_____

2. **Be a Friend of Sinners**—Our burden for the unsaved must go beyond the inward stirring of our heart. We must reach out to befriend those around us who are lost. Jesus set the example for us during His earthly ministry.

   How did He get to know people who were not saved (Matthew 9:10–13)?

_____

_____

What did His enemies accuse Him of being (Matthew 11:19)?

_____

_____

   As Christians, you and I are to be separated from ungodliness, but not necessarily separated from the ungodly. We need to live in this world, building friendships with those who need our Savior. We must not isolate ourselves but be the light that Jesus spoke of in Matthew 5:14–16. God wants us to be lights for Him. No amount of darkness can put out the smallest flame. We need to shine as lights in this world. There is no better way to do that than to befriend those who are lost.

How would you describe the light or witness that you are to be according to Matthew 5:14–16?

_____

_____

Where do you encounter unsaved people that God would want you to befriend?

3. **Be a Listener**—Jesus spent time in conversation with the publicans and sinners as He sat and ate with them. Because He had listened to them, when the opportunity came, they came close and listened to Him (Luke 15:1)! Do you hear and see the needs of those around you? Or are you so consumed with yourself that you cannot "hear" the searching cries from those who do not know our great God? We must learn to listen and then we will know when to respond.

How can you improve your listening skills?

4. **Be Saturated with the Word and Knowledge of Our Lord**— We will not be prepared to point others to God if we are not walking closely with Him. We need to live our lives in such a way that others can see Him in and through us. All the answers man will ever need for life and godliness are found in God's Word.

II Peter 1:2–4

Grace and peace be multiplied unto you through the knowledge of God, and of Jesus our Lord, according as his divine power hath given unto us all things that pertain unto life and godliness, through the knowledge of him that hath called us to glory and virtue: whereby are given unto us exceeding great and precious promises: that by these ye might be partakers of the divine nature, having escaped the corruption that is in the world through lust.

We may not have the time or opportunity to open our Bibles with someone, but we can open our hearts to effectively minister. Our love and knowledge of God and His Word need to control us so that our speaking of God is a natural part of our conversation.

What should our relationship be to our Lord according to these verses?

II Corinthians 5:20

We should be _____ for Him.

Philippians 1:21

We should _____ for Christ and be ready to _____ and be with Him.

Philippians 2:5

We should _____ as our Lord _____.

Philippians 3:10

We should know _____

      know His _____

      know His _____

      know His _____

      be made like Him in His _____

5. **Be Ready to Share**—Only God can draw a heart to Himself. However, He often uses a godly friend as an instrument to bring a lost soul to Himself. We must be prepared and willing to open our mouths to boldly speak the good news of the gospel.

Many passages can be used to lead someone to understand and accept salvation. Study the following verses and note the truths that will lead a person to accept Christ as Savior and give him or her assurance of salvation.

    Salvation—Romans 3:10

          Romans 3:23

          Romans 6:23*a*

          Romans 5:8

Romans 6:23*b*

Romans 10:9–10

Romans 10:13

See John 3:14–17 for further clarification.

Assurance—John 1:12

John 10:29

I John 1:9

It is helpful to

1. Write Romans 3:10 in the front of your Bible to remind you where to begin.
2. Write the next reference in the margin of your Bible; by Romans 3:10, write Romans 3:23. Follow this pattern throughout.
3. Practice with someone who is saved until you can go smoothly from verse to verse.

Just a Thought . . .

Around the Corner, Around the World

Around the corner, around the world
A soul needs Jesus—a soul who's never heard.
Let's take the good news;
Let's take God's living Word –
Around the corner, around the world.

Ron Hamilton (Majesty Hymns, p. 539)

That I May Know Him

1. Realizing my responsibility to share Christ with those around me, who am I currently befriending and witnessing to?

_____

_____

_____

_____

2. Who else has the Lord burdened my heart for? What steps should I take to befriend them?

_____

_____

_____

_____

3. Write out Ephesians 6:19–20. May it be my prayer!

_____

_____

_____

_____

_____

_____

_____

_____

From My Heart to Yours

My favorite place to vacation is on the coast of the Atlantic Ocean. It does not matter if I am on the coast of New Hampshire, where the water is cool in the middle of the summer, or if I am on the warm, white sandy beaches of Florida. I love to be near the ocean.

Recently my family and I spent a few days on Sullivan's Island a few minutes from Charleston, South Carolina. Sullivan's Island is a beautiful, residential area and lacks the commercialized flavor that many coastal cities delight in. The quiet beach is just a few minutes' walk from the house where we stay. The path to the beach is a trail lined with lush, green Carolina growth. Once you reach the beach, the sights are wonderful. You can see the skyline of Charleston Harbor to your right, Fort Sumter straight ahead, and the wide-open seas to your left. The scene is beautiful. But my favorite sight is the lighthouse that can be seen on James Island directly across the bay. The James Island and the Sullivan's Island lighthouses send their lights across the bay to guide the many ships going in and out of the harbor. The lighthouses stand tall and strong, consistently warning the ships of the dangers of the shoreline. Their lights cannot be hidden even on the darkest of nights.

You and I need to be such a light to the lives of those around us. When we know Christ as our Savior, His love should fill us so that all can see His marvelous love and grace. We each need to be a lighthouse of the good news of the gospel. We need to be pointing others to our Savior just as the Sullivan's Island lighthouse points the ships to safety. How does your light shine? Are you a clear beacon of the truths of God's Word to the people around you?

nine

MY GOD WHO HEARS
I Samuel 1:1–2:11, 19–21

The book of Samuel begins with Hannah, a woman who led a life that many would find impossible to patiently endure. Hannah carried a burden that we cannot imagine today— she had to share her husband with another wife. Although Hannah had the love of her husband, Elkanah, God had not given Hannah children. Peninnah, on the other hand, did not have Elkanah's love, but God had given her sons and daughters. The severe treatment and hateful words that Hannah received from Peninnah were unbearable. She constantly reminded Hannah of her childless state. In spite of Elkanah's continual reminders of his love, the mocking and scorn she constantly received from Peninnah devastated Hannah. Hannah found it difficult to eat and to stop the tears from flowing.

A Prayer of a Mother

Read these verses about Hannah and answer the questions. From the life of this dear lady, we will learn how God can take a broken but obedient heart and bless it beyond measure.

I Samuel 1:1–8

What three difficulties did Hannah face?

1. _____

_____

2. _____

_____

3. _____

_____

I Samuel 1:9–18

When Hannah went to God for comfort and help, what promise did she make to Him?

_____

_____

_____

I Samuel 1:17–20

When Eli understood Hannah's heart, what did he promise her?

_____

_____

_____

How did Hannah's response to Eli's promise change her actions?

_____

_____

_____

Her situation?

_____

_____

How did God fulfill Hannah's hope? _____

I Samuel 1:21–28

How did Hannah keep her promise to God? _____

_____

I Samuel 2:19–21

God blessed Hannah for her faithfulness to Him.

How?_____

When? _____

TRUTH #1
God Helps in Time of Need.

Time in the Word: Read I Samuel 1:1–18.

Hannah is an example of a godly woman who took her burden to God. She turned to God instead of continuing in her despair. In I Samuel 1:9, Hannah went to the temple in Shiloh and poured out her heart to God in silent prayer. "In bitterness of soul [she] prayed unto the Lord, and wept sore" (v. 10). Hannah made a vow to God as she prayed for a baby boy. She promised God that the child would be given to God "all the days of his life" and that no razor would "come upon his head" (v. 11). This promise shows that Hannah took the Nazarite vow for her desired son.

The Nazarite vow is explained in Numbers 6:1–6. What rules do these verses indicate for this vow?

1. _____

_____

2. _____

_____

3. _____

_____

4. _____

_____

What warning is given in Ecclesiastes 5:4–5?

_____

_____

_____

How does this vow show the sincerity of Hannah's promise to God?

_____

_____

_____

Hannah's prayer was so intense that although she did not speak aloud her lips moved. Eli falsely accused Hannah of being drunk. She explained to Eli that she had "poured out [her] soul before the Lord" (v. 15). Without even knowing the details of her request, Eli promised her that God had heard her prayer and that He would grant her request.

Hannah immediately changed. She left the temple with her burden lifted. Her circumstances, however, had not changed. She was not leaving with the promised son in her arms. Nor was the child in her womb. But she left rejoicing with the promise of God's answer! That is all Hannah needed—the promise of God!

Hannah returned to her home in Ramah with the assurance that God had heard her prayer. It was not long until the baby boy she had asked for was conceived and born. They named him Samuel, which means, "I have asked him of the Lord" (v. 20).

Our Refuge and Strength

Hannah found her help in God. In the following verses, the psalmist explains that "God is our refuge and strength, a very present help in trouble" (Psalm 46:1).

Match the verses with the description of God as our Help.

1. Psalm 33:20 _____
   Our soul waiteth for the Lord: he is our help and our shield.
2. Psalm 41:1 _____
   Blessed is he that considereth the poor: the Lord will deliver him in time of trouble.
3. Psalm 60:11 _____
   Give us help from trouble: for vain is the help of man.
4. Psalm 63:7 _____
   Because thou hast been my help, therefore in the shadow of thy wings will I rejoice.
5. Psalm 72:12 _____
   For he shall deliver the needy when he crieth; the poor also, and him that hath no helper.

A. God thinks of me and delivers me.
B. God keeps me safe in the shadow of His wings.
C. God helps when there is no one else to help.
D. God is my shield.
E. God helps in times of trouble.

A Prayer for Help

Psalm 56 is a prayer of David that shows the confidence we can have when we go to God for help. David gives us a comparison of his fear of his enemies and the faithfulness of his God. Your enemies and fears may be different from Hannah's or David's, but these promises from Psalm 56 can apply to any challenge and struggle.

As you read each verse of Psalm 56, note the description of David's God and/or his fears and enemies.

Psalm 56	God	David's Enemies/Fears
Verse 1	Merciful unto me	Man would swallow me up
Verse 2		
Verse 3	Trustworthy	
Verse 4		What flesh can do
Verse 5	_____	
Verse 6	_____	
Verse 7	God cast down in anger	
Verse 8		_____
Verse 9		

Verse 10	Praise His Word	_____
Verse 11		Man
Verse 12		_____
Verse 13		_____

Just a Thought . . .

In Mark 9:14–29, Jesus heals a man's son. The father asked Jesus, "If thou canst do any thing, have compassion on us, and help us" (v. 22). "If thou canst do any thing. . . ." What an incredible thing to say to God the Son! What could possibly be beyond the help of the Lord Jesus?

How many times do I go to God in prayer with the same questioning heart that this father had? There is no problem that I face that God cannot solve. Nothing is outside His power and concern. He promises to give me the grace to match my every need. He tells me to cast all my cares on Him because He cares for me (I Peter 5:7). The Lord Jesus would have me listen and heed the instruction He gave this man. "If thou canst believe, all things are possible to him that believeth." May the father's response be mine! "Lord, I believe; help thou my unbelief" (Mark 9:23–24).

That I May Know Him

1. What fears and enemies do I have in my life?

_____

_____

_____

2. How do these truths about God being my helper apply to me?

_____

_____

_____

3. Am I trying to help myself through the world's solutions, or am I trusting God for His help and deliverance? How do my actions prove what I am trusting in?

_____

_____

_____

ten

MY GOD WHO HEARS
I Samuel 1:1–2:11, 19–21

TRUTH #2
God Honors Biblical Child Training.

Time in the Word: Read I Samuel 1:19–23.

God answered Hannah's prayer for a baby boy. While she waited for his birth, she began to plan and prepare. The time they would have together would be short. She had to make every moment of the next two or three years matter to have him ready to live in the temple with Eli.

And that day finally came—baby Samuel was born. How she must have treasured every moment she had with him! She used every day to teach and train him, as God would have her to. When the day came to give him back to the Lord, Samuel was ready. Hannah took Samuel back to Shiloh and presented him to Eli. She had prepared him, as best she could, to serve God.

The Bible is clear on how to train children. Even if you are not a parent, there are many children and young adults that may be looking to you as a "spiritual parent." In Titus 1:4, Paul calls Titus his "own son after the common faith." You may not be aware of how many consider you their parent in the faith as Titus did Paul. You have a responsibility to set the godly example that will strengthen and encourage the ones watching you. Your influence may be what God will use to mold that young life for His glory.

Godly Influence

Training a child to walk in God's ways begins in the heart and life of the adult. The following verses teach us the parent's or mentor's responsibilities. Match the verse to the correct responsibility.

Passage

1. Deuteronomy 4:10_____
2. Deuteronomy 6:5_____
3. Deuteronomy 6:6–7_____
4. Deuteronomy 6:13_____
5. Deuteronomy 11:16_____
6. Deuteronomy 13:4_____
7. Proverbs 22:6_____
8. Ephesians 6:1–4_____

Parent's/Mentor's Responsibility

A. Love God with all heart, soul, might
B. Fear Lord, serve Him
C. Word of God in heart, teach to child in daily walk
D. Walk with fear; obey, serve, cleave to God
E. Fear God, teach children
F. Be careful not to serve and worship other gods
G. Provoke not children to anger; nurture, admonish them in the Lord
H. Train child in way he should go

Rather than going into detail about biblical child-rearing principles, our goal is to see God in the life of Hannah. Because Hannah walked with God, she was able to instill in Samuel the godly principles that enabled him to serve God at an early age. We can be overwhelmed with the task of teaching children obedience and helping them de-velop godly character. We must depend on God for His guidance and wisdom as we work with young lives. There comes a day when each child must accept or reject the biblical teaching he has received. Since God designed man with a will to chose, our children must chose.

But God is faithful. His promises are true. Proverbs 22:6 states, "Train up a child in the way he should go: and when he is old, he will not depart from it." The phrase "when he is old" refers to a "mature adult . . . The verse stresses the simple principle that education in the home forms the man throughout his lifetime" (King James Study Bible, p. 984). May we strive to give our children the training that will lead them to a lifetime of service and love for God!

You will see a contrast in the lives of these Bible children. Who had godly character and who did not? Note anything about their parents' example that may have influenced their direction.

I Samuel 2:12, 17; 3:11–14 _____

_____

I Samuel 8:1–3 _____

_____

I Samuel 17:12–20 _____

_____

II Timothy 1: 1–6, 13–14 _____

_____

Just a Thought . . .

"Truly the most valuable gift you can give your family is a good example" (George, p. 181).

Do you realize the impact your life has on those watching you? We sometimes get the truest glimpse of our influence by accident. When our children began to talk, much of their early vocabulary was parroting what they heard my husband or me say. When our oldest child was about fifteen-months old, she began to use a comical expression. With her big blue eyes full of wonder, she would point at something and say, "Look-a, look-a, look at that!" It would bring a smile to anyone close by. We wondered where she had come up with the phrase until one day I was pointing something out for her to see and I used a similar expression. She was only repeating what she had heard me say. As she, her sister, and her brother grew, I realized many times that their words and actions were just a mirror that reflected their father or me. What a sobering observation! They were hearing and seeing me even when I thought I was going unnoticed. Oh, that my life would so reflect my Lord that I could say with the apostle Paul,

"Be ye followers of me, even as I also am of Christ" (I Corinthians 11:1).

That I May Know Him

1. Whose example am I following?

_____

_____

_____

_____

2. Whether I am a mentor or a mother, am I giving children a godly example to follow? What attitudes and actions show my godly example?

_____

_____

_____

_____

3. What biblical responsibilities for parents or mentors do I need to improve upon?

_____

_____

_____

_____

4. Spend time in prayer asking God to make you a better parent or mentor to the children in your life.

eleven

MY GOD WHO HEARS
I Samuel 1:1–2:11, 19–21

TRUTH #3
God Honors Sacrifice.

Time in the Word: Read I Samuel 1:24–28.

Hannah remembered that God had given Samuel to her as she faithfully taught and trained him. When Samuel was weaned and ready to live in Shiloh, Hannah kept the promise she had made—she gave Samuel back to God.

What an incredible act of love and obedience! Hannah had vowed to give him back, but how difficult it must have been. Such a little boy to leave at the temple to live with and help Eli. What a sacrifice Hannah made as she returned her only son to God! Hannah's obedience did not go without reward. After Hannah gave Samuel to God's service, God gave Hannah and Elkanah five more children—three sons and two daughters.

As mothers, we must be willing to give our children to God. They belong to Him. He has given them to us to love, nurture, train, and teach for His glory. We must allow Him to work in their lives and to use them for His glory. It is easy to say that they are His, but quite another thing to completely surrender them to Him. Do we let go and let Him take them wherever and through whatever He desires for them? May we follow Hannah's example and give our most precious gifts from God, our children, back to Him.

Precious Gifts

Children are not the only precious gifts that God asks us to give back to Him. Sacrifice is "the forfeiture of something highly valued . . . for the sake of someone or something considered to have a greater value or claim" (*American Heritage Dictionary*). What else does God ask us to sacrifice or surrender to Him for His glory?

Passage	Gift to Sacrifice
I Samuel 15:22	
II Samuel 24:24	
Luke 14:26	
Luke 14:33	
Romans 12:1–2	
II Corinthians 11:24–31	
II Corinthians 12:7	

Ephesians 5:16	
Philippians 1:21	
Hebrews 13:15	
1 Peter 4:11	

The Ultimate Gift

Does the cost seem too great? Read Isaiah 53. This passage is a prophetic picture of Jesus as the ultimate sacrifice. Consider what the Lord Jesus did for you by answering the following questions.

Isaiah 53:1–2, 6

How did people respond to the message and person of the Messiah, the Lord Jesus?

_____

_____

Isaiah 53:3–5, 7

What did Jesus endure on the cross as the sacrifice for your sins?

_____

_____

Isaiah 53:5

What did this suffering bring to mankind?

_____

_____

Isaiah 53:7

How did Jesus respond to what He endured?

_____

_____

Isaiah 53:10–12

The word "yet" means "nevertheless, despite this" (*American Heritage Dictionary*). Despite all the sufferings that Jesus endured, God was pleased with His sacrifice and exalted Him as the Lamb of God. How is Christ exalted in these verses?

_____

_____

How does Hebrews 10:10–14 further explain what Christ accomplished on the cross?

_____

_____

_____

_____

Just a Thought . . .

Consider the words to this wonderful old hymn. Can you say that your heart and life are fully surrendered to the Lord?

Take My Life, and Let It Be Consecrated

Take my life, and let it be
Consecrated, Lord, to Thee;
Take my hands, and let them move
At the impulse of Thy love.

Take my feet, and let them be
Swift and beautiful for Thee;

Take my voice, and let me sing
Always, only, for my King.

Take my lips, and let them be
Filled with praises, Lord, to Thee;
Take my silver and my gold,
Not a mite would I withhold.

Take my love, my Lord, I pour
At Thy feet its treasure store;
Take myself and I will be
Ever, only, all for Thee.

Frances Havergal

That I May Know Him

List the gifts that God has given you. How does He want you to give those gifts back to Him?

My Gifts	I give them to God as I . . .

When you consider all that the Lord Jesus endured for you (Isaiah 53), your heart should be filled with gratitude and humility. Spend some time in prayer thanking Him and rededicating to Him all that you are and have.

twelve

MY GOD WHO HEARS
I Samuel 1:1–2:11, 19–21

TRUTH #4
God Deserves Our Focus and Praise.

Time in the Word: Read I Samuel 2:1–11.

It is difficult to comprehend the grief that Hannah felt when she left little Samuel in Shiloh with Eli. No doubt her heart broke as she waved goodbye to him. The trip back to Ramah must have seemed long and lonely to Hannah. The few years that he had been with her seemed like days as she thought back over them. Would he be able to take care of himself? Would he be frightened in the temple day and night? How would Eli be able to provide the love and compassion that someone so little would need? These and other questions must have flooded Hannah's mind. But instead of succumbing to the overwhelming fear of those unanswerable questions, Hannah chose to put her focus on God.

Instead of being filled with sorrow, Hannah's heart was filled with rejoicing in God. First Samuel 2:1–10 gives us Hannah's prayer of praise offered to God. Her pride was not in her courage to obediently leave behind this little boy. Her delight was not in the glory of Samuel, although her heart must have been consumed with thoughts of him as they separated. Her jubilation came from the thought of her God; God had not only graciously given her a son but He also had given her the grace to give that son back to Him.

Hannah's Prayer

Hannah's prayer proclaims her heart of praise. We can see other verses that also emphasize the rejoicing that Hannah offered. As you read Hannah's prayer, also note the other verses that match her topics of joy. How do the other verses glorify God?

I Samuel 2:1—The Lord is a God of S _____

Psalm 9:14— _____

_____

2:2—The Lord is a God of H _____

_____

Exodus 15:11— _____

_____

2:2—The Lord is a God of S _____

_____

Psalm 18:2— _____

_____

2:3—The Lord is a God of K _____

_____

I Samuel 16:7— _____

_____

*2:4–8—The Lord is a God of P*_____

_____

Psalm 21:13— _____

_____

2:9–10—The Lord is a God of J _____

_____

Psalm 96:13— _____

_____

Psalms of Praise

The last five psalms speak of the praise that Hannah had for God that day. Prayerfully read them and then answer the questions.

*Psalm 146—*What has God done that deserves our praise?

_____

_____

_____

_____

Psalm 147—How does the psalmist describe God's greatness?

_____

_____

_____

Psalm 148—Who should praise God?

_____

_____

Psalm 149—What part does music have in praising God?

_____

_____

_____

Psalm 150—For what are we to praise God (v. 1–2)?

_____

_____

_____

How are we to praise God (v. 3–6)?

_____

_____

_____

Just a Thought . . .

I Thessalonians 5:18

In every thing give thanks: for this is the will of God in Christ Jesus concerning you.

When trouble comes, it is not easy to give thanks. Whatever touches my life is God's will for me. This verse says that "in every thing" I'm to give thanks. That means it is not for me to choose which events to be thankful for and which ones not to be. I'm to praise Him for all that touches my life. Even when times are difficult or discouraging, I can always praise God for who He is—my Savior and Lord!

A friend shared a video with me of a man preaching with this verse as his text. The young man exemplified this verse in an incredible way—he had cerebral palsy.

Just to walk to the pulpit was a grueling task, and each word he spoke took unbelievable effort. Yet, this godly man stood and praised God because he understood that God's will for him was to have cerebral palsy. His words were full of genuine gratitude and glory to God. Oh, that my life would be full of praise to my glorious God!

That I May Know Him

No matter what my circumstances are I can praise God! All else pales in comparison to His greatness.

1. What should I be praising God for today?

_____

_____

_____

_____

2. What has He done for me?

_____

_____

_____

_____

3. What do I know about Him that should make me praise Him?

_____

_____

_____

In Revelation we read that God alone is worthy of our focus and praise. Make these verses from Revelation your prayer of praise today.

Revelation 4:11

Thou art worthy, O Lord, to receive glory and honour and power: for thou hast created all things, and for thy pleasure they are and were created.

Revelation 5:12

Worthy is the Lamb that was slain to receive power, and riches, and wisdom, and strength, and honour, and glory, and blessing.

From My Heart to Yours

The wedding was beautiful. All the events that led to that day were precious and right. She was a beautiful bride marrying a wonderful Christian young man. Yet as I straightened the wedding gown that lay across my daughter's bed, the tears came. Where had the years gone? Kindergarten seemed only yesterday, but really college was what she had finished just a few months before. She should be that little blonde, blue-eyed girl I had put on the school bus seemingly days ago. But I knew in my heart that she really had become a lovely young woman.

As a mother of three beautiful children, I am called to search my own heart as I think of the life of Hannah. What an incredible sacrifice she illustrates for us! We catch a glimpse of the gift from God that children are as we carry them in our womb and then see them born. But as the years pass, it is easy to forget they are God's. With all the time, effort, and care that we put into their lives, it's easy to begin to think they are ours. But at what point do we have the right to claim them? Are they not still God's no matter their age?

It's not easy to admit they are growing up. We work and pray and teach with the goal of seeing those children grow to be godly, well-balanced, capable adults. And yet when they reach that point, how hard it is to believe the years have passed. Our children never completely belong to us. They are on loan to us from God. He gives them to us to love, train, and nurture. Oh, that we could be like Hannah and daily give them back to God. He alone knows what is best and right for them. He alone will be with them wherever they are. He alone must be the voice that they ultimately follow. We must not waste a minute, but instead use each day to teach them of God's love and goodness. Cherish each moment.

Notes

Hagar

King James Study Bible (Nashville: Thomas Nelson Publishers, 1981), p. 1424.

Thomas E. Ward, *Learning to Worship His Name* (Partners in Ministry, n.p., 1994), p. ii.

The Woman at the Well

Ron Hamilton, "Around the Corner, Around the World," *Majesty Hymns* (Greenville, S.C.: Majesty Music, 1996), p. 539.

King James Study Bible (Nashville: Thomas Nelson Publishers, 1981), p. 1613.

New Strong's Expanded Dictionary of the Words in the Hebrew Bible (Nashville: Thomas Nelson Publishers, 2001), p. 115.

Hannah

Elizabeth George, *A Woman's High Calling* (Eugene, Ore.: Harvest House Publishers, 2001), p. 181.

King James Study Bible (Nashville: Thomas Nelson Publishers, 1981), p. 984.

The American Heritage Dictionary (New York: American Heritage Publishing Co., 1973), p. 1141.

The American Heritage Dictionary (New York: American Heritage Publishing Co., 1973), p. 1484.